WHAT GOES ON INSIDE YOUR BRAIN?

EMOTION AND YOUR BRAIN

ROBERT SNEDDEN

Gareth Stevens PUBLISHING

Please visit our website, **www.garethstevens.com**.
For a free color catalog of all our high-quality books,
call toll free 1-800-542-2595 or fax 1-877-542-2596.

Cataloging-in-Publication Data
Names: Snedden, Robert.
Title: Emotion and your brain / Robert Snedden.
Description: New York : Gareth Stevens Publishing, 2019. | Series: What goes on inside your brain? | Includes glossary and index.
Identifiers: ISBN 9781538235690 (pbk.) | ISBN 9781538235706 (library bound)
Subjects: LCSH: Emotions--Juvenile literature. | Brain--Juvenile literature.
Classification: LCC BF531.S64 2019 | DDC 152.4--dc23

First Edition

Published in 2019 by
Gareth Stevens Publishing
111 East 14th Street, Suite 349
New York, NY 10003

Produced by Calcium
Editors: Sarah Eason and Claudia Martin
Designers: Paul Myerscough and Jeni Child

Photo credits: Cover: Shutterstock/unairakstudio. Inside: Shutterstock: Aleshyn_Andrei: p.1; Alex Mit: p.5; Andrii Vodolazhskyi: p.9; Antonio Guillem: p.36; Catalin Petolea: p.7; clkraus: p.25; decade3d/anatomy online: p.8; DenisProduction.com: p.3, p.26; DiversityStudio: p.4; fizkes: p.40; goodluz: p.18; goran cakmazovic: p.41; Irina Kozorog: p.14; isaac jose sanchez meza: p.31b; koya979: p.6; Lapina: p.12; logoboom: p.35; Lucky Business: p.44; mimagephotography: p.28; Monika Wisniewska: p.27; Monkey Business Images: p.21, p.22, p.38; MriMan: p.29; muzsy: p.23; Nattakorn_Maneerat: p.43; Oksana. Bondar: p.13; Ollyy: p.10; oneinchpunch: p.30–31; Pete Broyles: p.33; Photographee.eu: p.39; PitK: p.11; pixelheadphoto digitalskillet: p.42; Rawpixel.com: p.17, p.45; Romaset: p.24; Sabphoto: p.37; sanjagrujic: p.34; Sebastian Kaulitzki: p.15; Stefan Holm: p.32; Tatyana Dzemileva: p.16; Tewan Banditrukkanka: p.19; wk1003mike: p.20.

Printed in the United States of America

CPSIA compliance information: Batch #CW19GS
For further information contact Gareth Stevens, New York, New York at 1-800-542-2595.

CONTENTS

CHAPTER 1

THE HUMAN BRAIN

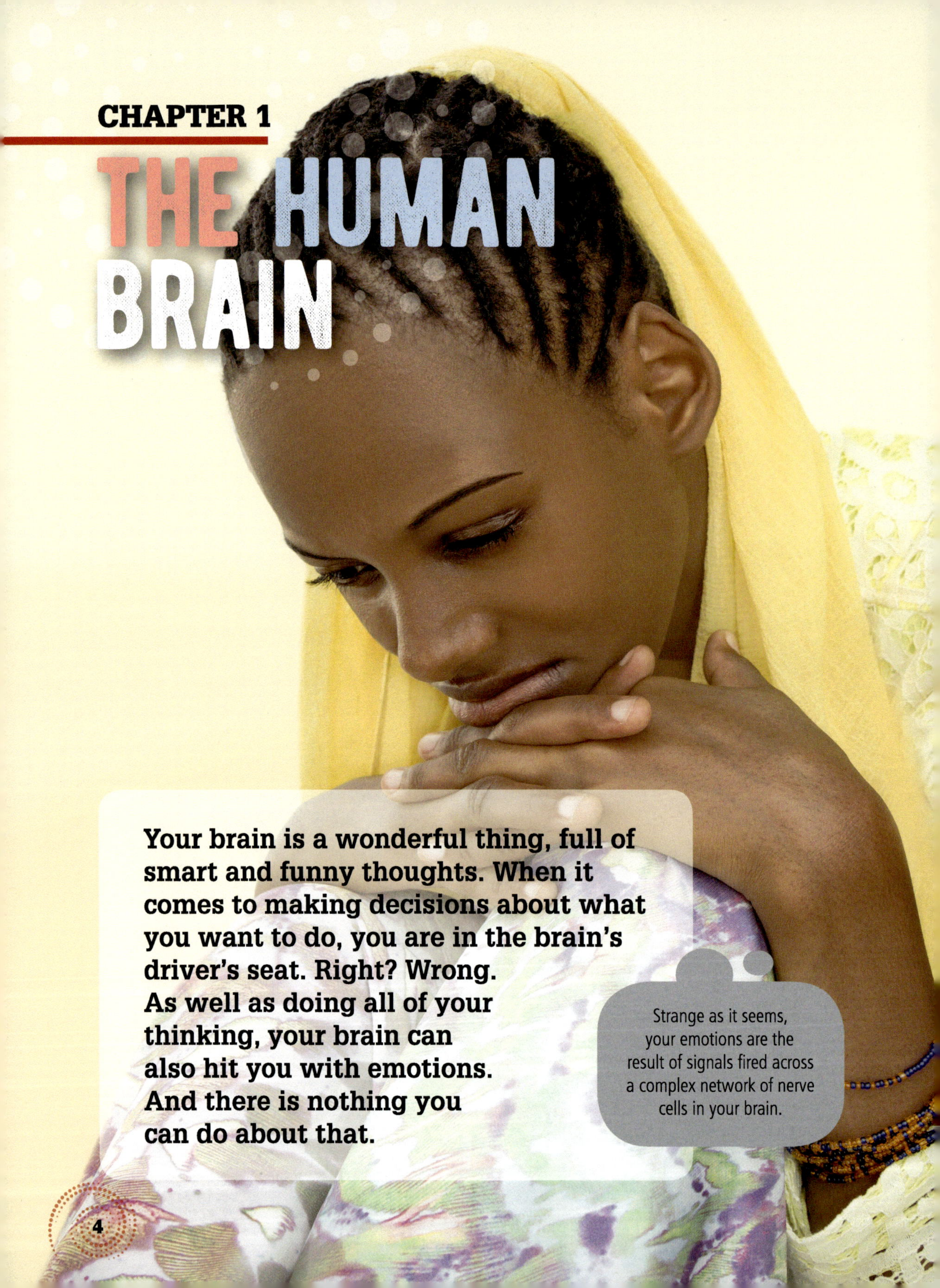

Your brain is a wonderful thing, full of smart and funny thoughts. When it comes to making decisions about what you want to do, you are in the brain's driver's seat. Right? Wrong. As well as doing all of your thinking, your brain can also hit you with emotions. And there is nothing you can do about that.

Strange as it seems, your emotions are the result of signals fired across a complex network of nerve cells in your brain.

In many ways your brain is you. This is where all your thoughts are, your hopes and fears, your imagination, and your emotions. No one knows just exactly how it all works, but teams of scientists and doctors around the world are working tirelessly to find the answers.

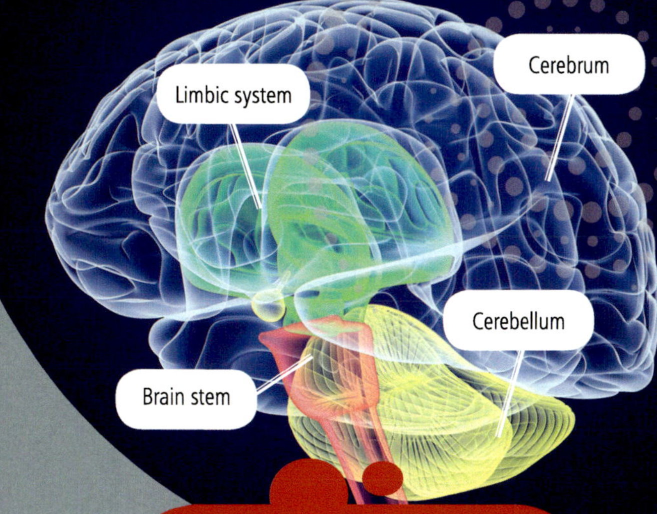

The brain is divided into different structures, all working together to keep you alive and make you who you are.

Brain Cells

Your brain is made up of two types of cell. The first type are called neurons, or nerve cells, which are the brain's communication network. Neurons vary in shape and size, but the largest neurons in the brain are no more than 1/250 of an inch (0.1 mm) across. Each neuron can be linked to thousands of other neurons, through connections called synapses. Signals are constantly being fired through the synapses. The second type of cell are glial cells. These surround neurons and hold them in place, supply the neurons with oxygen and nutrients, and remove dead neurons. In addition, scientists now believe that glial cells may also take part in the brain's thought processes.

INSIDE YOUR BRAIN

The average brain weighs about 3 pounds (1.4 kg). It has around 100 billion neurons, connected to each other through perhaps 60 trillion synapses. Scientists disagree about the number of glial cells, but recent estimates also put the number of glials at roughly 100 billion.

Brain cells are organized into different structures, each with its tasks to perform. At the rear of the brain is the hindbrain, which includes the cerebellum and parts of the brain stem. These control the body's vital functions, such as heart rate and breathing. At the center of the brain is the limbic system, which is closely linked to emotions and strongly influences our behavior. Surrounding the limbic system is the cerebrum, which coordinates input from the senses and is where we do our conscious thinking.

The Thinking Brain

The outer layer of the cerebrum is called the cerebral cortex. This is where our language skills, our imagination, and our conscious thoughts are found. The cerebral cortex is divided into two hemispheres, left and right. Each hemisphere consists of four areas called lobes:

- The frontal lobe is the area involved with planning and with control of the emotions.
- The parietal lobe is responsible for processing some information from the senses, including touch and temperature.
- The temporal lobe processes signals from the ears and is involved with language recognition and memory.
- The occipital lobe is responsible for processing vision.

The right and left hemispheres of the brain are joined by a bundle of fibers that carry messages from one side to the other. Each hemisphere controls the opposite side of the body, so the left hemisphere of the brain controls the right-hand side of the body.

Each hemisphere doesn't do exactly the same thing as the other. In general, the left hemisphere controls skills such as speech, writing, and mathematics ability. The right hemisphere is in charge of artistic and musical skills as well as creativity.

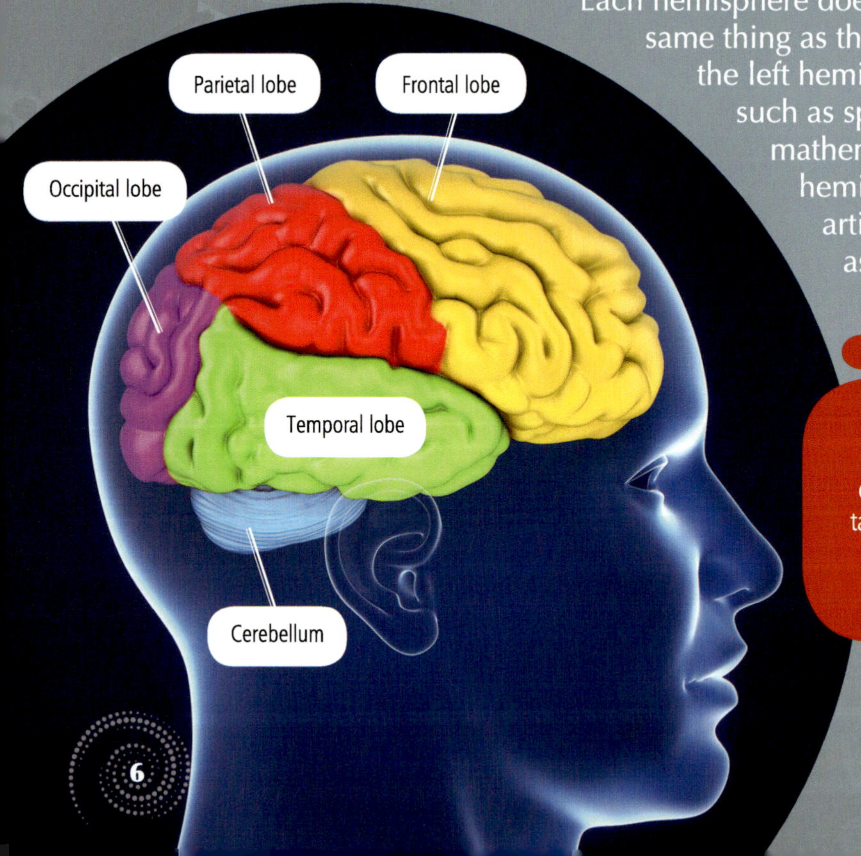

The cortex of the brain is divided into four lobes, each with a different set of tasks to perform. We rely on all the lobes working efficiently together.

If something makes you afraid you shouldn't ignore it: There may be a good reason for your emotion.

Overruling the Emotions?

All the different parts of the brain communicate with one another all the time. It is not always an equal partnership, however. Have you ever heard someone say, "My emotions got the better of me"? In many ways, that can be true. There are far more pathways bringing messages from the emotional part of the brain, the limbic system, to the thinking part than there are going in the opposite direction. The thinking cortex might try to keep our emotions in check, but it does not always work.

SPEAK YOUR MIND

Why do you think it might be important that we can't always overrule our emotions? Think about how you need to act if something makes you afraid. Are there some emotions that it would be useful to overrule? Give reasons for your answers.

CHAPTER 2

THE SIX EMOTIONS

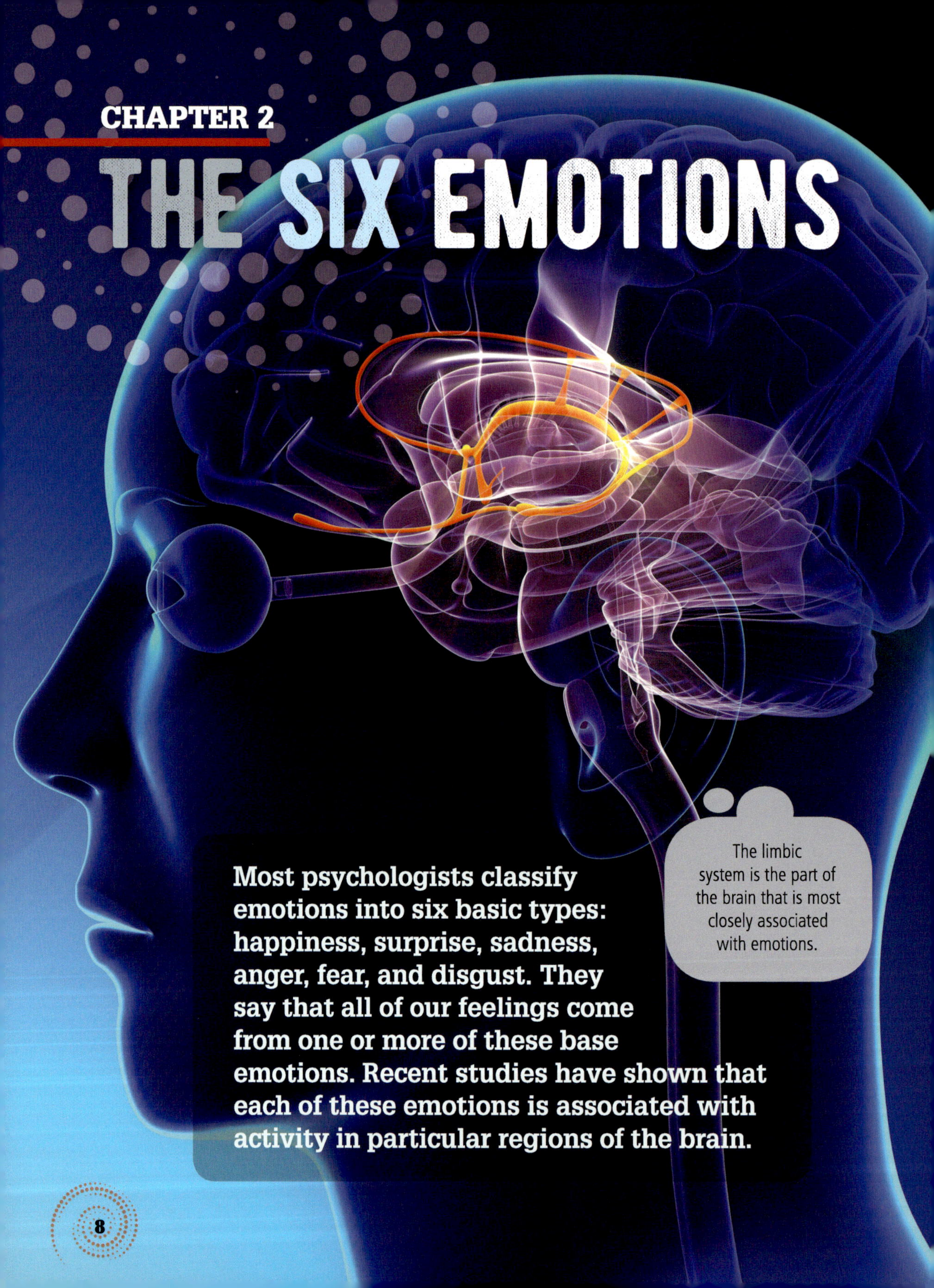

The limbic system is the part of the brain that is most closely associated with emotions.

Most psychologists classify emotions into six basic types: happiness, surprise, sadness, anger, fear, and disgust. They say that all of our feelings come from one or more of these base emotions. Recent studies have shown that each of these emotions is associated with activity in particular regions of the brain.

Some researchers believe that other emotions, such as pride, guilt, or embarrassment, are really made from the building blocks of the six basic emotions. Embarrassment, for instance, could be seen as a combination of sadness that you did something wrong, and anger that you were found out.

Which Emotion Where?

One part of the brain that is involved in most of our emotions is the amygdala, an almond-shaped collection of nerve cells in the limbic system. You actually have a pair of amygdala, one in each hemisphere. Once considered to be involved mainly with fear and other negative emotions, the amygdala is now known to play a part in more positive feelings, too. For example, happiness is associated with activity in the amygdala and the cortex, the thinking part of the brain. Sadness is linked to increased activity in the occipital lobe, amygdala, and hippocampus, which is also in the limbic system and is strongly connected with memory.

Sometimes a surprise can be pleasant, but at other times it is totally the opposite. Surprise is the only emotion that does not appear to involve the amygdala. Surprise is something you associate with experiences that are unexpected, or which you do not recall having happened to you before. This is probably why surprise causes activity in the hippocampus, the region associated with memory.

INSIDE YOUR BRAIN

Emotions are controlled by dozens of chemical messengers, called neurotransmitters, in your brain. By adjusting the levels of these neurotransmitters, your brain determines how you respond to events and can change your mood. If you are in danger, for example, messengers are released that speed up your reactions, increasing your chances of getting safely away.

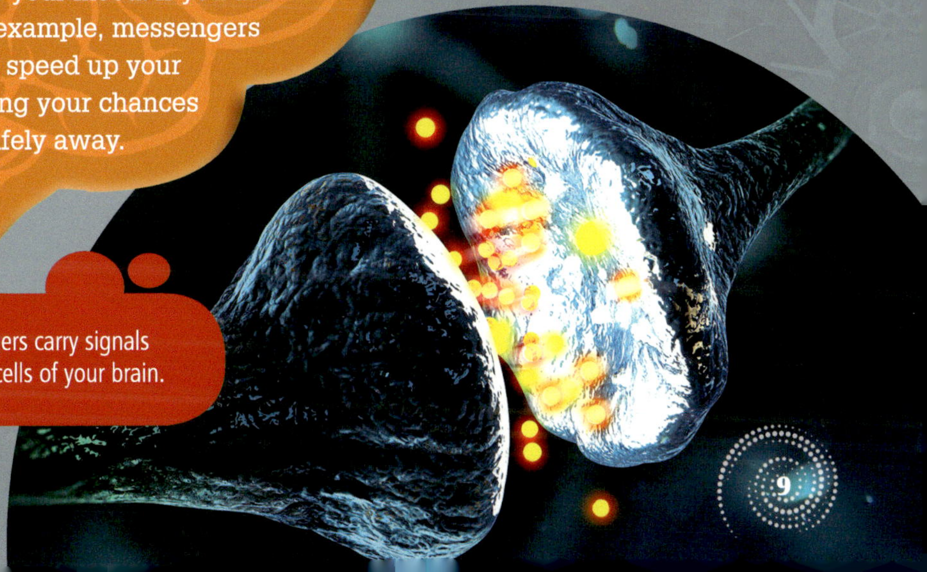

Chemical messengers carry signals between the nerve cells of your brain.

More Than Six Emotions?

The idea that we have six basic emotions has been accepted for decades. But lately some researchers have been challenging this idea. Some have suggested that, rather than six, we have 27 different emotions.

Just how many different emotions are there? Is boredom an emotion, or contentment?

In 2017, researchers at the University of California, Berkeley got together 850 volunteers and split them into three groups. Then they got them to watch video clips that were intended to produce different emotional responses. The first group were allowed to say in their own words how the clips made them feel. The second group had to rank the videos against 34 categories of emotion supplied by the research team. The third group had to rate the videos on a scale according to how exciting, or scary, or disgusting, and so on, they found them.

After analyzing the data they gathered, the researchers came up with a list of 27 emotions. Among them were awe, confusion, horror, sadness, and triumph. Interestingly, one thing that was not on the new list was anger. Fear and envy were there, but not anger. As well as identifying far more emotions than before, the researchers also took another step away from the "six basic emotions" theory. Emotions, they decided, were all connected to one another and, for example, horror and sadness could blend into each other.

Fewer Than Six Emotions?

On the other hand, researchers at the University of Glasgow, in Scotland, took a different point of view. They looked at the way the muscles in the face move when we are expressing different emotions. They decided that, since both fear and horror share a similar wide-eyed look, they should be considered as one basic emotion, not two. In addition, when we feel anger or disgust, our noses wrinkle, so perhaps they are just one basic emotion, too.

The Glasgow researchers were not suggesting that anger and disgust do not exist as separate emotions. Their theory is that there are four basic emotion building blocks—anger, fear, happiness, and sadness—and more complex varieties of emotion, such as disgust or embarrassment, have evolved from these.

SPEAK YOUR MIND

Think about all the different ways you are capable of feeling. Do you think that they can all be built up from the six basic emotions? Can you think of an emotion that isn't made from a combination of two or more of the six? Give reasons for your answers.

Fear can make you look wide-eyed, but so can horror and surprise.

CHAPTER 3

DO WE NEED EMOTIONS?

The way we behave is always influenced by the emotions we feel. Emotions also guide us in managing and planning our lives—as when we make snap decisions based on "gut instinct." How we react emotionally to any event allows us to decide whether it is something we want to avoid, or to enjoy.

Sometimes you feel fear in the movie theater, but does fear serve a purpose?

It is almost impossible to imagine what an emotionless life would be like. Emotions play a role in forming the attitudes, values, and beliefs that guide how we feel and act in the world and with the people around us. The emotions we attach to our beliefs give them value to us. How deeply would you believe something that made you feel nothing? At the same time, emotion can cloud our judgment. You may have heard someone say they were so angry they "couldn't think straight."

Part of the American Psychological Association's definition of emotion describes it as a response to a situation that is "perceived to be personally significant." In other words, we only get emotional about things that mean something important to us.

Emotions for Survival

You might have noticed that the "good" emotions (happiness and, sometimes, surprise) are outnumbered by the "bad" ones (fear, sadness, disgust, and anger). This may be a clue to why we have emotions at all. Perhaps the fact that there are more "bad" emotions indicates that, for our ancestors, and indeed for us, survival was more important than having fun!

Emotions allow us to react rapidly, without conscious thought, to sudden changes in our surroundings. If you taste something disgusting, you spit it out right away without stopping to think about it. Your body is warning you that you might be about to eat something that will make you sick, and the emotion of disgust you feel makes you act instantly.

SPEAK YOUR MIND

Think about the four negative emotions: sadness, anger, fear, and disgust. Can you think of situations when having those emotions would help you to survive? It may be hard to understand how feeling sad could help you to survive, but think about how different the world would be if no one ever felt sadness. Give reasons for your answers.

There is no mistaking the facial expression of someone who is disgusted!

The Power of Fear

You are lying in bed late at night, drifting off to sleep. It is dark and quiet. Suddenly, there's a loud crash. You sit up. Your heart is racing. Sweat breaks out on your forehead. What are you going to do? Then you hear another sound and you relax. It's just the neighborhood cats arguing over the trash can.

You have just experienced fear—perhaps the most important emotion of them all. It is so important because, more than any other, it is the one that will be most likely to keep you alive. The emotion of fear brings about a sense of dread, alerting you to the possibility of danger and getting you ready to protect yourself.

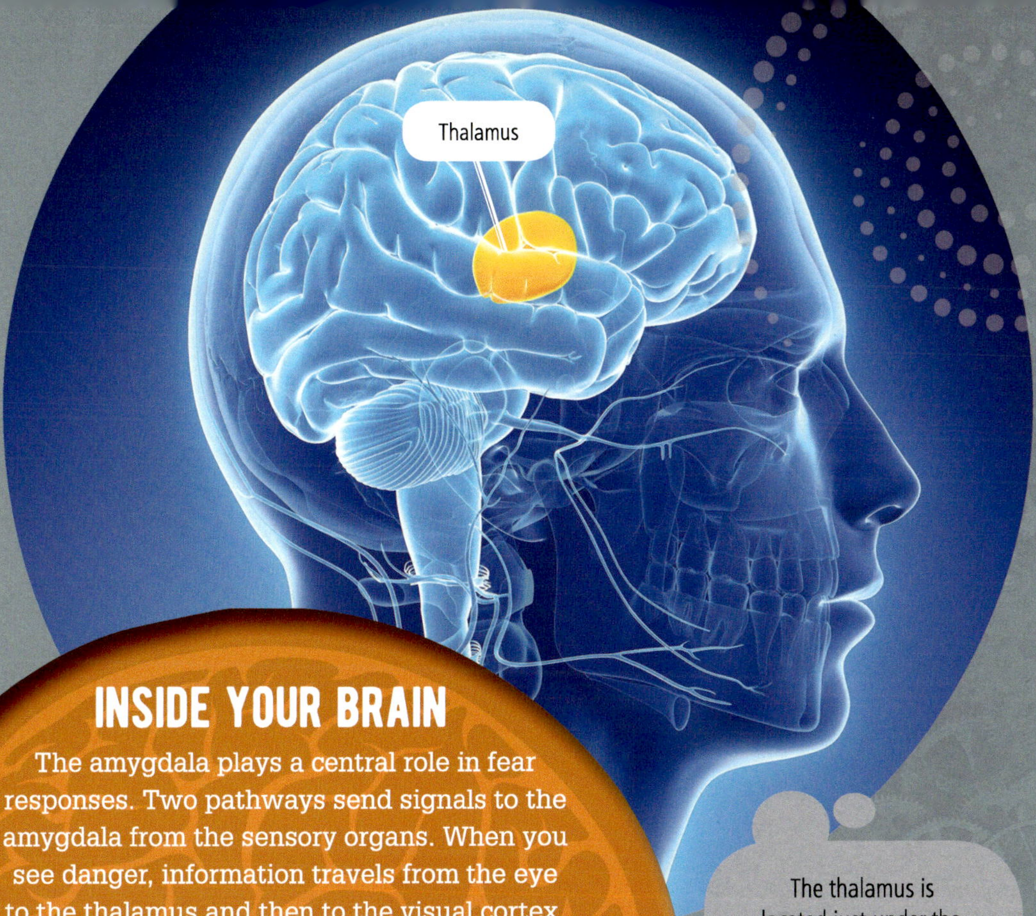

The thalamus is located just under the cerebral cortex. Nerve fibers run from the thalamus into the cortex in all directions. The thalamus is the brain's main processing center for information from the senses.

INSIDE YOUR BRAIN

The amygdala plays a central role in fear responses. Two pathways send signals to the amygdala from the sensory organs. When you see danger, information travels from the eye to the thalamus and then to the visual cortex, which sends the information on to the amygdala. However, the thalamus also quickly sends the information straight to the amygdala, so that you can react to the danger before you are even consciously aware it is there.

Fight or Flight

The response to fear is often referred to as a "fight or flight" reaction. It isn't just humans that show this response. When confronted by a threat, many animals will either get ready to stand their ground and fight it out or run as fast as they can to put distance between them and danger.

Another response to fear shown by humans and other animals is to "play dead," or freeze, when threatened. This response most likely evolved as a way of demonstrating that you were harmless and thus not worth attacking.

Sending Emotional Messages

The feeling of disgust is an example of the way emotion affects us as individuals. It triggers a response that is not dependent on what anyone else is doing. However, a second important role played by emotions is in interpersonal relationships—the way we act toward one another. When we are with other people, we are sending out signals all the time, indicating our moods and feelings. Most of the time, we are not even doing this consciously.

Emotions and the expressions they cause to appear on our faces send information to the people we are talking to about our feelings toward them, what we might be intending to do next, and how comfortable we feel about the situation we are in. No text message emoji can communicate the way a person is feeling the way the expression on their face can.

Emojis are fun, but they can't communicate emotion like a real human face.

A smile sends a signal that you are among friends and happy.

INSIDE YOUR BRAIN

Experiments have shown that, when we look at faces, a region of the brain located behind each ear, named the posterior superior temporal sulcus (pSTS), becomes active and immediately identifies facial expressions. However, only the pSTS on the right side of the brain activates. No one is sure why.

We need to have a good idea how we expect other people to behave if we're going to work well together. Because emotions have such an important role to play in the way people act toward one another, we learn to control them in certain situations. We learn, for example, to stop having the sort of temper tantrums we had as infants every time we don't get what we want right away.

Bonding

Another important aspect of emotion is how feeling the same emotion as others helps us to bond with them. Have you ever been at a great concert and seen your own joy reflected on everybody else's face? When we are really happy, we often laugh. You may have noticed how laughing together plays a vital part in bonding and helps to ease tensions between individuals. Even feeling negative emotions together, such as sadness, plays a role in holding together families, friendships, and even whole countries. We feel supported when we see that others feel just the same way.

CHAPTER 4

WHERE DO EMOTIONS COME FROM?

Are emotions something we are born with or are they something we learn, like how to read? The traditional view is to see emotion as hardwired into the brain. In this way, for example, when events trigger the circuit for happiness, responses are set off in the body, causing the appropriate facial expression to appear. But are there other explanations?

People who have been blind from birth use exactly the same muscles to smile as sighted people.

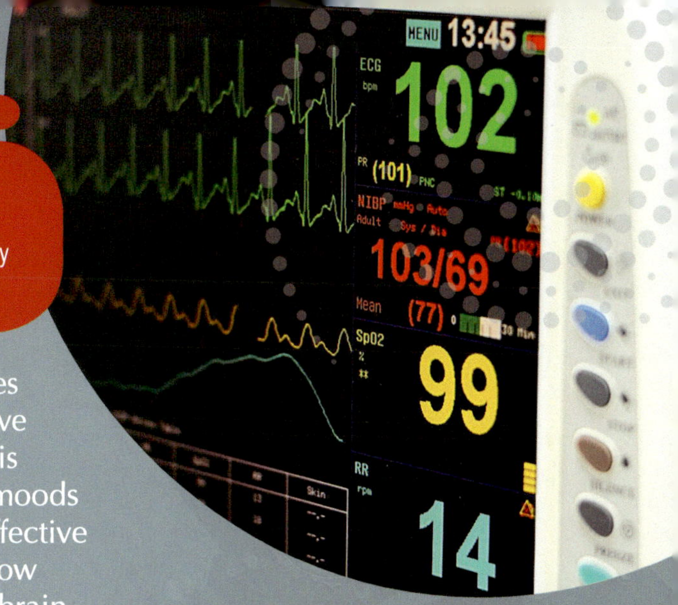

A heart monitor can measure the increased heart rate of someone who is afraid or under stress. Everyone's body responds the same way when they experience these emotions.

The study of the way the brain creates emotional responses is called affective neuroscience. An affect, in science, is an emotional process and includes moods and feelings, as well as emotions. Affective neuroscience wants to understand how emotions arise from activities in the brain.

Built-In Facial Expressions

As far as most neuroscientists are concerned, emotions are the automatic and unconscious reactions the body has to events, such as the fast heart rate and dry mouth we experience when we are afraid, or the way our eyes widen when we are surprised. They say that the facial expressions of emotion are built in and common to everyone.

Research carried out in recent years seemed to back this up. San Francisco State University researchers analyzed nearly 5,000 photos to compare the facial expressions of sighted and blind judo athletes from 23 countries at the 2004 Summer Olympics and Paralympic Games. The researchers were able to demonstrate that sighted and blind individuals use the same muscles to produce the same facial expressions when responding to specific emotional events.

It had been suggested previously that infants learned to match facial expressions to emotions by watching what others did. But the San Francisco researchers showed that this could not be the case, since people who were blind from birth would be unable to learn about expressions.

INSIDE YOUR BRAIN

The brain circuits responsible for generating emotions are deep within the brain, below the cerebral cortex. Specific emotions are not located in a single structure of the brain. Networks of structures throughout the brain become active during any emotional process.

Emotional Noises

The situation appears to be a little different with emotional sounds, however. A team of researchers from the Netherlands asked eight deaf and eight hearing people to make the sounds they associated with different emotions, including anger, fear, disgust, and sadness, but without using words.

Next, the researchers played back the recordings to 25 hearing individuals and asked them which emotion they thought each sound matched up to. When they listened to the sounds produced by the hearing people, they found it easy to match sound to emotion. However, with the sounds made by the deaf people, only laughter and a sigh of relief were easily identifiable.

These findings suggest that the sounds we commonly associate with most emotions are not hardwired—they must be learned. However, laughter is a universal communication signal between people. This almost certainly shows what an important part laughter plays in our lives.

You can only see this little girl and not hear her, but you can probably still make a good guess at her emotion!

It's Good to Laugh

Laughter plays a vital part in bonding people together and helps to ease feelings of stress and anxiety. Laughter can even override other emotions. You will very likely know from your own experience that it is nearly impossible to stay angry once you find something funny. There are several brain circuits involved in laughter. For example, activity in the parts of the brain involved in controlling our behavior and decision-making is temporarily dialed back so we feel less inhibited. The brain circuits linking the areas of the brain responsible for experiencing emotion with those involved in expressing emotion are also active when we laugh.

SPEAK YOUR MIND

How do you think that people who are deaf from birth can learn to laugh? Do you think it is possible to copy the way another person laughs even if you cannot hear them? Take a look at a video clip of someone laughing with the sound turned down to try it for yourself! Do you think laughing is an important skill? Give reasons for your answers.

Feeling Pleasure

We all like to feel good. One of the most rewarding experiences our brains can give us is to trigger the emotion of happiness. Looking for that reward motivates us to be enthusiastic and interested in what is going on around us.

Several regions of the brain appear to be involved in this "desire system." They include the hypothalamus, the amygdala, and the front part of the frontal lobe of the cortex. They are activated by a neurotransmitter called dopamine, produced in specialized circuits in the brain. Dopamine creates a sense of excitement, meaningfulness, and anticipation.

Research has discovered that the left frontal lobe is more active than the right during emotions such as desire and interest. The pleasure we get from sweet things seems to be inbuilt. Scans using equipment such as electroencephalograms (EEGs) have shown increased left frontal lobe activity in infants as young as two to three days old when a drop of sucrose is placed on their tongues. Hungry adults just have to look at a picture of a tasty dessert to get the same response!

Just looking at a tasty treat can activate the brain's pleasure centers!

Is the pleasure of winning that soccer trophy as strong as the desire to win it?

Looking for Reward

We show how much we want something by the amount of effort we are prepared to put into getting it. We show how much we like what we get by our happy facial expression, among other things. It might surprise you to know that the interest you have in getting a reward does not have to correspond to how much you like the reward you get. This is because the parts of your brain involved in the enjoyment of a reward are different from those involved in the desire to get the reward.

Research about enjoying rewards has found that a small area within a part of the brain called the nucleus accumbens is involved. When we do something rewarding, dopamine levels rise in this part of the brain. Oddly, they also appear to rise when we experience something negative. Scientists are still trying to figure out exactly what this area of the brain does.

SPEAK YOUR MIND

How does it make you feel to know that your strong desire to get on the track team, get an A on a test, or see the latest movie is all caused by the firing of nerve cells in the frontal lobe and limbic system? Does this make you desire those rewards more or less? Give reasons for your answers.

Equipment such as an electroencephalogram can be used to monitor electrical activity caused by the neurons in the brain.

Feeling or Emotion?

It is very easy to confuse feelings with emotions. In our everyday language, we often use the terms as if they mean the same thing —and indeed they are closely connected with each other.

For the neuroscientist, emotions are physical changes triggered in the brain by events taking place around us. Feelings are what we experience after the conscious brain becomes aware of these physical changes. Emotions happen in your body; feelings happen in your mind. You do not feel afraid, for example, until you become consciously aware of the activity taking place in your body, such as the dryness in your mouth and your pounding heart. It can take just a split second for this awareness to take place.

Essentially, emotions are inbuilt and instinctive: an instant reaction to the possibility of a threat or reward. You cannot do anything about them, as they are just the way your body is wired to respond to certain situations. They are produced by a part of your brain that is not controlled by logic or reason. Emotional reactions do vary slightly between different people, but by and large emotions are similar across all humans.

Feelings, on the other hand, are what the reasoning part of our brains makes of these emotions. Your emotional brain might have you ready to make a run for it—but you don't have to. Feelings are prompted by emotions, but they are also affected by memory. The way you reacted to a particular emotion in the past will influence the way you react to it now. Feelings are the meanings your thinking brain attaches to your emotions.

INSIDE YOUR BRAIN

Emotions are a physical process and can be measured using recording devices that monitor things such as pupil dilation (the width of the pupil of the eye), heart rate, and brain activity. Feelings, on the other hand, can only be assessed by asking a person to report on how they feel. There is no guarantee that what they are telling you is true!

When you are startled, you respond instinctively and immediately—you throw down that towel and leap away from the spider! This is an emotional reaction, not a feeling.

CHAPTER 5

READING EMOTIONS

We can often tell what mood another person is in. By looking at the expression on someone's face and their posture (the way they hold themselves), we can sometimes tell right away if they are happy, sad, or angry.

Knowing what mood someone is in guides us in the way we respond to that person. If the other person is really angry, it might not be the right time to do something silly! There's no one way of displaying a particular emotion, so it is often easier to judge the emotion of someone you have a lot of experience with than someone you have just met.

If you saw children looking unhappy at a party, you would soon be wondering what had gone wrong.

It seems that we can also learn which emotions to attach to which events. If it's a happy occasion, like a birthday party, we expect the people taking part to be happy. There are lots of different ways for people to show they are happy, so our memory that birthday parties are happy helps us out when our brains are guessing what other people are feeling.

Hard to Pretend

To some extent, we can try to fake our emotions. An actor in a movie will only be pretending to be angry in a scene. Actors are much better at pretending emotions than the rest of us—generally, it is hard to do it convincingly. You can usually spot when someone is pretending to smile, for example, as it is next to impossible to control the muscles around the eyes that a genuine smile uses. Body language and tone of voice may give the game away, too.

INSIDE YOUR BRAIN

The amygdala plays a major role in identifying emotions. When we look at a face, brain cells in the amygdala fire off electrical impulses. One group of cells, the emotion-tracking neurons, detect a single specific emotion, such as happiness or fear. A happiness-signaling neuron sends out more impulses if we see a happy face, for example. Another group of cells, the ambiguity-coding neurons, respond if we're not too sure what the other person is feeling. These neurons appear to play a part in what we eventually decide about the other person's mood.

Actors try to fake emotions, but we are quick to spot when they do not do it effectively.

What's on Your Mind?

Although we are pretty good at guessing what kind of mood another person is in, it is impossible to know what they are really thinking. However, scientists are trying to take steps in that direction! Researchers have used a machine called a functioning magnetic resonance imaging (fMRI) scanner to monitor activity in the brain. People being tested had to lie down inside a large tube while the machine used powerful magnetic forces to measure the changing activity of the brain cells in different areas of the brain.

Making Mental Maps

The scientists got their test subjects to watch a movie or listen to music that would trigger different emotions. The fMRI allowed them to build up a series of "mental maps" showing what was going on in the brain when the subject reported feeling a particular emotion, such as fear or happiness.

It is sometimes difficult to know what someone is thinking about. Perhaps that is a good thing.

In the next stage of the experiment, the scientists invited their test subjects to just lie in the scanner and think about anything they wanted to. They did not do anything to try to influence the person's emotional state. The researchers wanted to know if the scanner would detect fleeting changes of emotion depending on what crossed the person's mind.

The test subjects were questioned at regular intervals and asked about their current emotional state. At the same time, data from brain scans were collected every few seconds and compared with the brain maps of emotion from the previous experiment. When the researchers examined the scans taken a few seconds before the person was asked about their mood, they found that the brain patterns they had recorded were good at predicting the emotions the test subjects reported.

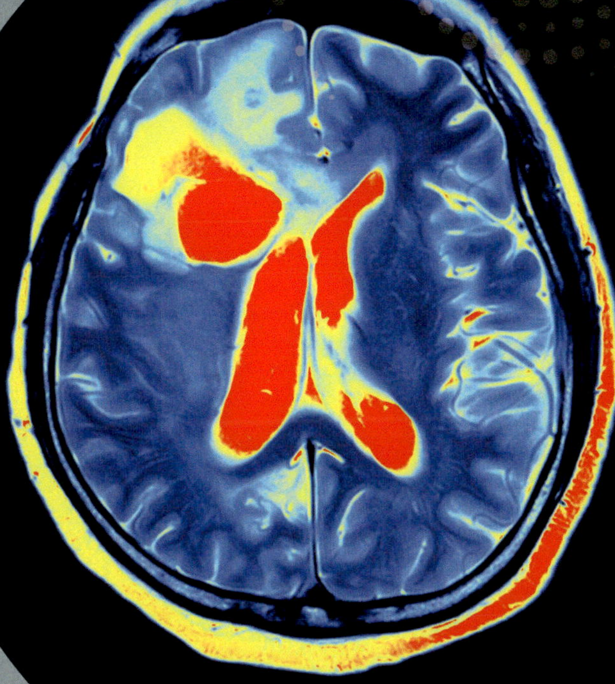

Researchers used fMRI scans to show changing levels of activity in the brain with different emotions.

SPEAK YOUR MIND

Imagine that technology developed to the point where machines could identify not just emotions but actual thoughts. Do you think that such a machine should be used, and under what circumstances? Or do you think that some things should always be private? Give reasons for your answers.

Do We All Feel the Same Way?

If you traveled to another country, you might expect the people there to like different types of food to the specialties you enjoy. You wouldn't be surprised to find them speaking a different language. But would you expect the people there to have the same emotions as you do—and express them in the same way?

We all feel the same emotions, but our culture and upbringing can lead us to express them in different ways.

Differences in Expression

Does a person's culture affect the way they respond emotionally to different situations? Does it determine what makes them happy, or what makes them sad? Today, most researchers agree that there are some differences across cultures. For example, culture seems to play a big part in the way people think about themselves. People from North America, for instance, tend to think of themselves as individuals, whereas people from East Asia see themselves as more connected to others. When researchers asked American and Japanese students to complete the sentence, "I am…" 20 times, the American students were more likely to say how they felt ("I am happy"), whereas the Japanese students were more likely to say what their place in society was ("I am a student").

Studies of the way people respond to emotional events look at three different aspects: how the body responds (for example, increase in heart rate); what the person says they are feeling; and what their facial expression is. By and large, whatever a person's culture, their bodies react in the same way. The difference is in the way the emotion is expressed on their faces. North Americans tend to be more likely to express their

emotions openly, perhaps as a way of influencing how others feel, whereas East Asian people tend not to show their emotions so much, perhaps so as to fit in with everyone else. They may also be less willing to say how they are feeling.

There seem to be both similarities and differences in the way people of different societies interpret the facial expressions associated with emotions. For example, people from the United States tend to focus on the mouth when interpreting other people's emotions, whereas people from Japan tend to look at their eyes.

SPEAK YOUR MIND

Think about your own background. What have you been told at home and at school about the way you express your emotions? How does this make you feel about yourself and the way you behave toward others? How do you expect them to behave toward you? Give reasons for your answers.

Japanese anime characters have expressive eyes, reflecting the way Japanese people tend to judge the emotions of others.

CHAPTER 6

EMOTION AND MEMORY

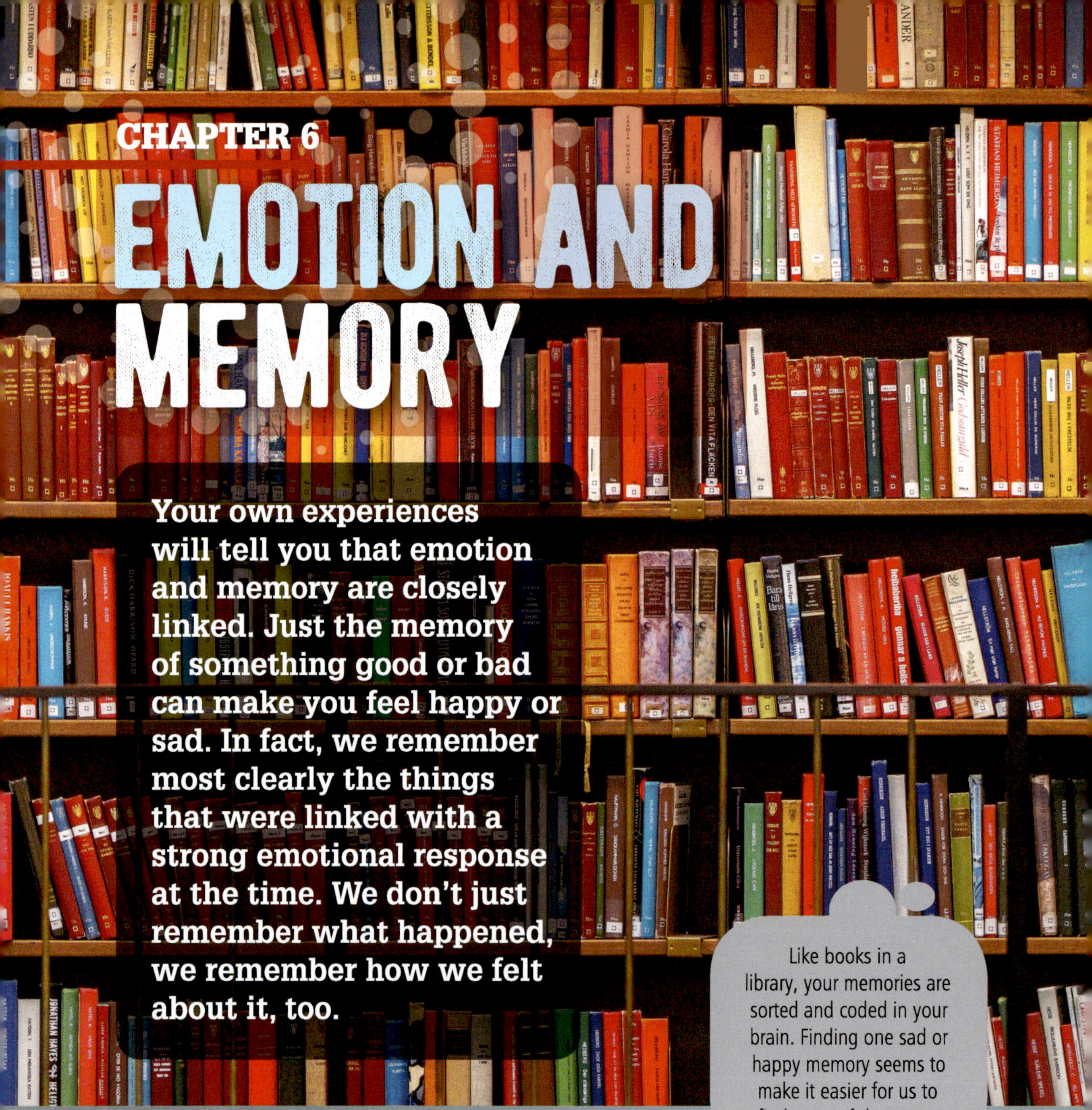

Your own experiences will tell you that emotion and memory are closely linked. Just the memory of something good or bad can make you feel happy or sad. In fact, we remember most clearly the things that were linked with a strong emotional response at the time. We don't just remember what happened, we remember how we felt about it, too.

Like books in a library, your memories are sorted and coded in your brain. Finding one sad or happy memory seems to make it easier for us to find more of the same.

Memories are very rarely just facts stored randomly in our brains. Like books on the shelves of a library, they are coded and labeled, in this case with the emotions we felt at the times the memories were formed. When you are happy, you will most likely find it easier to remember other times when you were happy. When you are sad, other sad times will come more readily to mind.

Flashbulb Memories

A person's emotional state at the time an event occurs can affect how it is stored in their memory. Researchers sometimes refer to what they call "flashbulb memories." These are when people are able to recall with great detail where and what they were doing when an event of great significance occurred, such as the terrorist attack on the World Trade Center on September 11, 2001. Flashbulb memories tend to occur only when the event is felt to be of particular importance to a person or when it causes a state of shock or surprise.

INSIDE YOUR BRAIN

As we have seen, the amygdala plays a central role in our emotions. Next door to the amygdala is the hippocampus, which is involved with memory. Researchers believe that the two brain regions communicate with each other so memories from the hippocampus reinforce the way we react to an event if it happens again. For example, smelling something that reminds us of a past experience may also trigger the emotional response we had at the time.

The smell of freshly baked cookies may always remind us of making cookies as a child, making us feel happy all over again.

People suffering from Alzheimer's disease may find it takes their emotions longer to return to normal after an upsetting incident.

The Feeling Remains

In a recent experiment, researchers from the University of Iowa showed a group of volunteers a series of video clips that had been specially selected to trigger feelings of sadness or happiness. Half the group of volunteers were healthy adults, but the other half were people who suffered from Alzheimer's disease. Alzheimer's disease, which mainly affects older people, causes severe memory loss. It largely affects the cortex, the thinking part of the brain. This means that sufferers may have less control of emotional parts of the brain, such as the amygdala.

When questioned afterward, the Alzheimer's patients could recall few details of the clips they had watched, even though just minutes had passed. In fact, four of the patients could not remember any details about the videos, and one had no recollection of watching anything at all. However, the Alzheimer's patients reported feeling happy after watching the happy videos and sad after watching the sad videos. These feelings persisted for up to half an hour after the viewing.

There was even some evidence to suggest that the less the person remembered about the video, the longer the emotion associated with it lasted. A possible explanation for this was that, because the brain could find no reason for the feeling, it kept going back to it and examining it, causing it to persist for longer.

Recovering from Emotions

A similar study looked at the link between "memory performance" (how well people recall experiences of a specific time or place) and "emotion recovery" (how quickly they return to a normal state following an emotional event). Participants were shown video clips showing scenes of sadness and loss, while the researchers watched how they reacted and recovered over time. It was discovered that older adults with intact memory skills could return to a normal emotional state faster than those with Alzheimer's disease.

SPEAK YOUR MIND

What do you think this research about Alzheimer's disease tells us about memory and emotion? Does what you have read shed any light on your own memories and emotions? How long does it take you to recover from upsetting events? Perhaps you think it is not always possible to completely recover. Give reasons for your answers.

CHAPTER 7

EMOTIONAL WELL-BEING

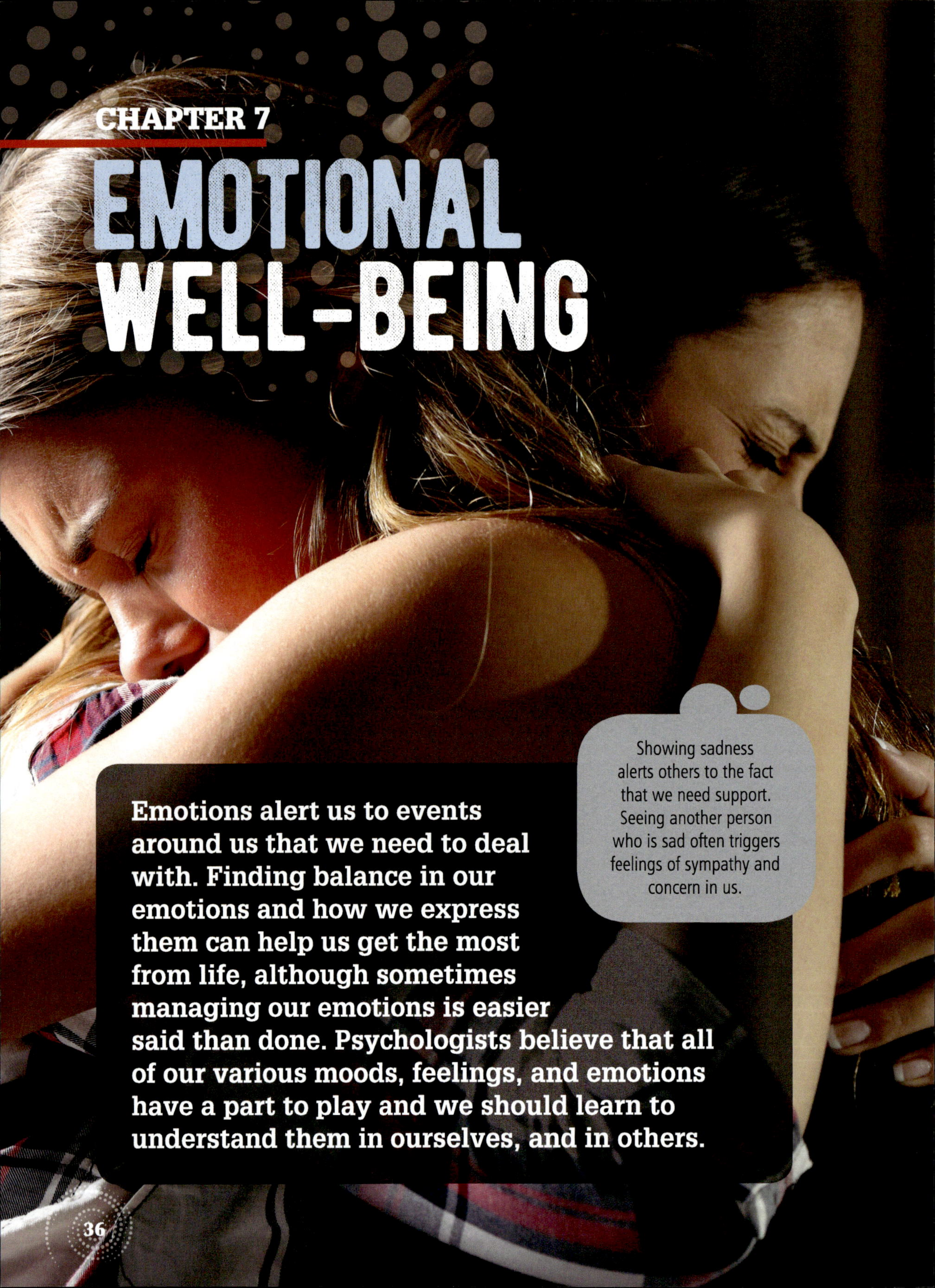

Showing sadness alerts others to the fact that we need support. Seeing another person who is sad often triggers feelings of sympathy and concern in us.

Emotions alert us to events around us that we need to deal with. Finding balance in our emotions and how we express them can help us get the most from life, although sometimes managing our emotions is easier said than done. Psychologists believe that all of our various moods, feelings, and emotions have a part to play and we should learn to understand them in ourselves, and in others.

There are always going to be times in our lives when we feel sad about something.

As we have seen, positive emotions and feelings are greatly outnumbered by the negative ones. But the negative emotions are undeniably useful because they help us to avoid situations that could be harmful and dangerous. Perhaps the most common of the negative emotions is sadness. What could possibly be the benefits of feeling sad?

A temporary sad mood may help us to cope with everyday challenges and difficult situations. Usually some event in our lives triggers the feeling of sadness. Looking sad sends a signal to others that we are no longer fully engaged with what is going on around us. When we appear sad, it triggers feelings of concern in others and makes them inclined to help.

Depression

If a feeling of sadness persists over a long time, it becomes depression. Depression is a serious, and common, mental disorder. A depressed person may feel sad about everything. Some people who suffer from depression describe themselves as not feeling anything at all, not feeling happy or sad but just numb. Researchers believe that depression—and other mental illnesses—may partly be a result of the brain's inability to attach appropriate emotions to events. The hope is that, as research deepens our understanding of how the brain processes emotions, new therapies for depression will be found.

INSIDE YOUR BRAIN

Recent research has involved investigating nerve channels from the amygdala that carry information about pleasant or unpleasant events. It is possible that the way this information is routed, and sometimes misrouted, could help to explain why some people suffer mental illnesses, including depression, addiction, and anxiety.

Fear or Anxiety?

As we have learned, fear serves the purpose of keeping us safe. The differences between fear and anxiety can be confusing. Both fear and anxiety are triggered by things we feel threatened by. Fear is generally considered to be a reaction to something that threatens your safety right here and now, such as an unexplained noise in the night.

Anxiety, on the other hand, is a general feeling of distress or unease that is longer lasting than fear. Things we commonly refer to as fears, such as a fear of flying or a fear of heights, are actually anxieties. Anxiety makes you wary of some threat or danger that might lie in the future, whereas fear is a response to threat or danger that has to be dealt with immediately.

Feeling anxious now and then is a perfectly normal part of life. You might feel anxious if you are about to start a new school, or if you have a difficult test to take. But this feeling is temporary and will go away once you have done what you had to do. For a person with an anxiety disorder, however, the anxiety does not go away and may often get worse.

It is natural to feel anxious when we have to deal with something that worries us.

People suffering from PTSD benefit from therapy that helps them to replace distressing thoughts with positive ones.

Anxiety Disorders

There are several different types of anxiety disorders. For example, people with panic disorder have unexpected panic attacks, a sudden feeling of intense fear that makes them shake and tremble, with pounding heart and shortness of breath. People with social anxiety disorder are fearful of offending others, are afraid of social situations, and fear that they will be made to feel embarrassed or rejected.

Post-traumatic stress disorder (PTSD) is a type of emotional anxiety that can follow experiencing an event that caused extreme fear, such as wartime combat, a natural disaster, or a serious accident. It can be months after the event before the symptoms appear. These include severe anxiety and panic, and reliving the event, often with the same degree of fear as the person felt during the event itself. People with PTSD become withdrawn, show less emotion, and lose interest in things that were once important to them.

SPEAK YOUR MIND

Everyone feels anxious now and then. What do you do when you feel anxious? Have you developed a strategy for coping with anxiety? Ask other people what strategies they have. Give reasons for your answers.

We all get in a bad mood now and then, but maybe that's the time to get some work done!

Good to Feel Bad?

You probably think that being in a bad mood is not the best frame of mind for tackling a difficult homework assignment. But you might be wrong. Some research has shown that feeling bad can sometimes be good. Investigators at the University of New South Wales, in Australia, found that, while performing a task, people who were in a bad mood paid more attention to detail, were less likely to make errors of judgment, and were more likely to come up with high-quality arguments than people who were in a good mood.

It was also discovered that, when happy and sad participants were asked to perform a difficult mental task, those in a bad mood tried harder and would keep working on the problem for longer than the people who were happy. When being tested, they not only attempted more of the questions, but also came up with more correct answers.

Coming to Terms with Negative Emotions

Another investigation looked at the way adults of different age groups responded to certain emotional circumstances. Groups of older adults, aged from 60 to 92, and younger adults, aged from 18 to 32, were presented with lists of words associated with emotions. It was found that older adults saw words such as "sadness" and "loneliness" in a more positive light than younger people did. The older adults were more comfortable with the idea of sadness than the younger ones, perhaps because they had learned to accept "bad" emotions as a natural part of life.

INSIDE YOUR BRAIN

Researchers have found evidence that suggests people who are experiencing negative emotions—fear, anger, disgust, or sadness—make better eyewitnesses to crimes. Being in a bad mood appears to reduce a person's likelihood of being distracted by false or misleading information.

Older people appear better able to deal with feelings such as loneliness and sadness than younger people.

Emotional Intelligence

Emotional intelligence (EI) examines the relationship between thinking and emotion. It is certain that our emotions influence our day-to-day behavior in a big way, including the way we relate to other people and how we make decisions. Seen from an EI standpoint, if we develop the right tools, we can keep control of our emotions. But just how do we go about doing that?

EI researchers describe EI as the ability to monitor your own feelings and those of others and to use that information to guide your actions. One branch of EI breaks it down into four steps: 1: perception/expression of emotion; 2: using emotion to guide your thinking; 3: understanding of emotion; 4: managing emotion in yourself and others.

Developing EI

Perception of emotion is about the ability to identify emotions using such clues as facial expressions, tone of voice, and body language. People who are good at the perception of emotion tend to be good at expressing emotion, too.

Some emotional states are better for achieving what you want than others. Using emotion to improve your thinking and your ability to adapt to changing situations is the second part of EI. People who are skilled at this actively generate emotions that support certain tasks or objectives. For example, getting psyched up for a football game is a different mindset from the calm you need to sit down and write an essay.

Before a game, football players work up the aggressive emotions they need to be competitive.

Being able to distinguish between different emotional states and what brought them about is another EI skill. Getting caught in the rain when you are on your way somewhere can be a bit annoying. Standing in line for hours in the rain only to discover that the event you wanted to see has sold out can leave you feeling angry and frustrated.

Part of managing emotion includes recognizing the value of feeling certain emotions in particular situations, understanding which strategies are best at regulating emotion, and being open to a wide range of emotion. In some situations, anger may be an unavoidable response, but it is good to take time to calm yourself down to avoid anger leading to aggression.

SPEAK YOUR MIND

How useful do you think it would be to develop your emotional intelligence? Do you think it would make it easier to get through life? Or do you think it is best to speak your mind at all times? Give reasons for your answers.

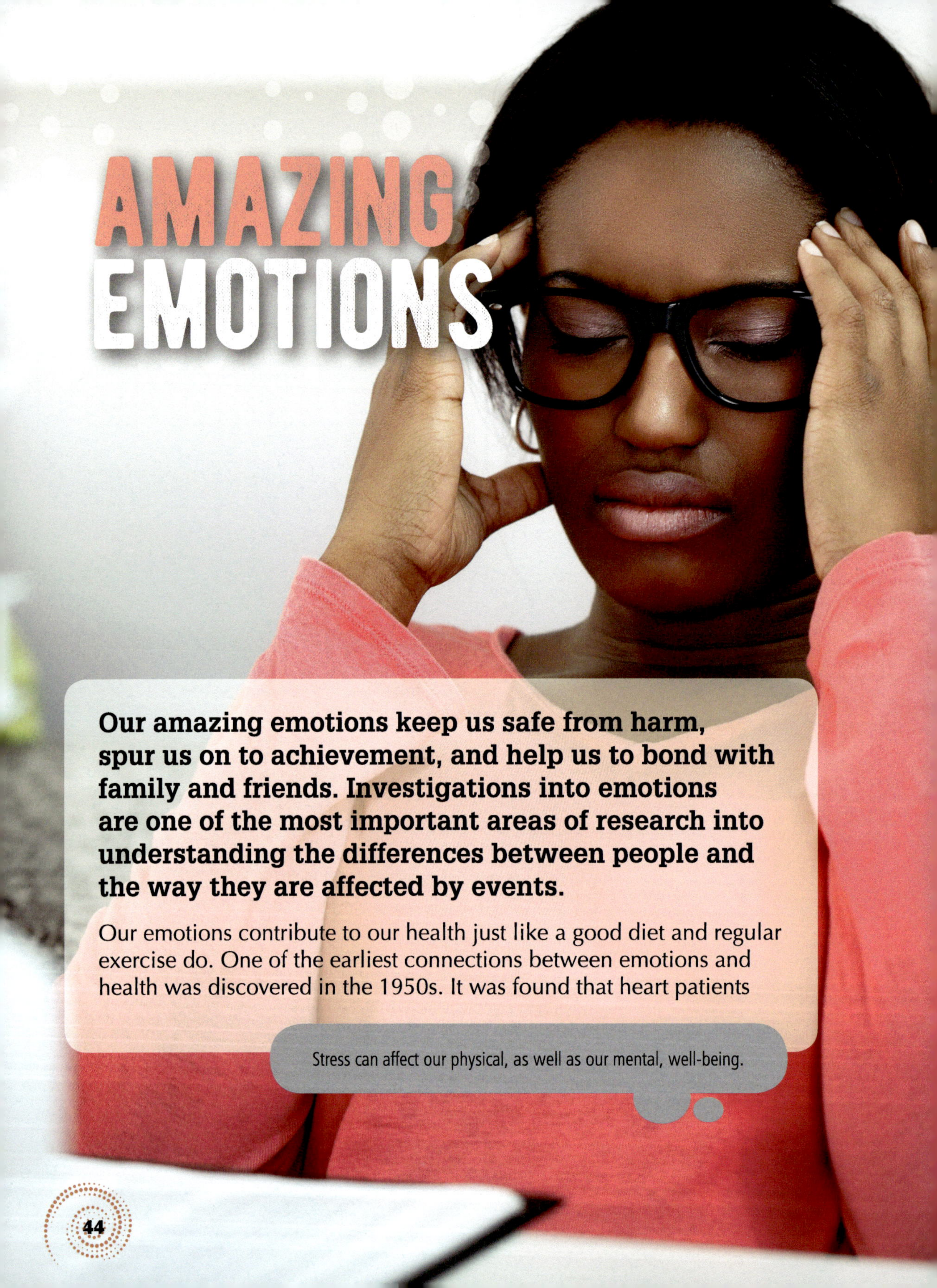

AMAZING EMOTIONS

Our amazing emotions keep us safe from harm, spur us on to achievement, and help us to bond with family and friends. Investigations into emotions are one of the most important areas of research into understanding the differences between people and the way they are affected by events.

Our emotions contribute to our health just like a good diet and regular exercise do. One of the earliest connections between emotions and health was discovered in the 1950s. It was found that heart patients

Stress can affect our physical, as well as our mental, well-being.

often showed behavioral patterns that were less common in other patients. These included being competitive, impatient, hostile, and being a "clock watcher."

People who are hostile are, as you are probably aware, quick to get angry and upset. Frequent anger can actually cause damage to the arteries in the heart. Also, because hostile behavior tends to drive others away, hostile people often lack a protective social network that would help them to deal with stress and ill health.

Look on the Bright Side

In contrast, a positive outlook can have positive benefits for health. In all cultures, even in areas considered to be poor and deprived, positive emotions are linked with better health, including a better chance of recovery from illness and of living longer.

An optimistic outlook has been shown to improve our ability to cope with the problems that inevitably come our way in life. About 20 percent of Americans report experiencing stress at some point, with 18- to 33-year-olds reporting the highest levels. Positive emotions can protect us from the damaging effects of stress and even prevent it altogether. So always look on the bright side!

SPEAK YOUR MIND

Think about periods in your life when you have felt unhappy or stressed. Did you also feel physically unwell? Are you convinced by the argument that acting positively can have a positive effect on your health? Give reasons for your answers.

Having fun with family and friends not only makes us feel happy, it also has benefits for our overall health.

GLOSSARY

amygdala Part of the limbic system in the brain; it is particularly associated with emotions.

brain stem The part of the base of the brain that controls our heartbeat and breathing.

cell One of the building blocks of life; different types of cells are specialized to carry out different tasks in the body.

cerebellum The area at the back of the brain that controls the working of our muscles.

cerebral cortex The outside layer of the cerebrum that is used for many key functions and is where thinking takes place.

cerebrum The largest part of the human brain.

electroencephalograms (EEGs) Machines that can detect the tiny electrical impulses produced by the neurons in the brain.

emotional intelligence (EI) The ability to be aware of, control, and express emotions.

functioning magnetic resonance imaging (fMRI) scanner A machine that takes detailed pictures of the inside of the body.

glial cells A type of cell found in the brain, which supports the neurons.

hippocampus A horseshoe-shaped area in the limbic system involved with memory.

hypothalamus A part of the limbic system that regulates sleep, hunger, thirst, and affects some behaviors.

limbic system An inner region of the brain involved with instinct, mood, and emotion.

lobe A curved or rounded part of something. Each hemisphere (half) of the brain is divided into four lobes: frontal, parietal, occipital, and temporal.

neurons Nerve cells.

neuroscience The study of the brain and the nervous system.

neurotransmitters Chemicals that carry signals from one nerve cell to another.

post-traumatic stress disorder (PTSD) A severe condition caused by horrible experiences and memories.

psychologists People who study the human mind.

thalamus A part of the brain involved in relaying information from the senses.

FOR MORE INFORMATION

Books

Abramovitz, Melissa. *Brain Science*. Minneapolis, MN: Essential Library, 2016.

Brukner, Lauren. *The Kids' Guide to Staying Awesome and in Control.* Philadelphia, PA: Jessica Kingsley Publishers, 2014.

Meister, Cari. *Totally Wacky Facts About the Mind*. North Mankato, MN: Capstone Press, 2016.

Weeks, Marcus. *Heads Up Psychology.* New York, NY: DK Publishing, 2014.

Websites

Discover the different parts of the brain at:
ducksters.com/science/brain.php

Read more about fear, anxiety, and the brain at:
kidshealth.org/en/kids/afraid.html?WT.ac=ctg

Find out more about understanding and managing your emotions at:
kidshealth.org/en/teens/understand-emotions.html

Learn more about the brain at:
www.dkfindout.com/us/human-body/brain-and-nerves/inside-brain/

PUBLISHER'S NOTE TO EDUCATORS AND PARENTS:

Our editors have carefully reviewed these websites to ensure that they are suitable for students. Many websites change frequently, however, and we cannot guarantee that a site's future contents will continue to meet our high standards of quality and educational value. Be advised that students should be closely supervised whenever they access the Internet.

INDEX